Anne Morrow Lindbergh

THE UNICORN

AND OTHER POEMS

1935–1955

PANTHEON

COPYRIGHT © 1956 BY ANNE MORROW LINDBERGH

PUBLISHED BY PANTHEON BOOKS INC.

333 SIXTH AVENUE, NEW YORK 14, N.Y.

PUBLISHED SIMULTANEOUSLY IN CANADA BY

MCCLELLAND & STEWART, LTD., TORONTO, CANADA

ACKNOWLEDGMENTS:

THE ATLANTIC MONTHLY, THE SATURDAY REVIEW

FIRST PUBLISHED SEPTEMBER, 1956

1ST–10TH THOUSAND AUGUST, 1956
11TH–25TH THOUSAND AUGUST, 1956
26TH–50TH THOUSAND SEPTEMBER, 1956

LIBRARY OF CONGRESS CATALOG CARD NUMBER:

56–9810

MANUFACTURED IN THE UNITED STATES OF AMERICA

CONTENTS

LOVE

DEATH

6

LOVE

The Man and the Child

It is the man in us who works;

Who earns his daily bread and anxious scans
The evening skies to know tomorrow's plans;
It is the man who hurries as he walks;
Finds courage in a crowd; shouts as he talks;
Who shuts his eyes and burrows through his task;
Who doubts his neighbor and who wears a mask;
Who moves in armor and who hides his tears.
It is the man in us who fears.

It is the child in us who plays;
Who sees no happiness beyond today's;
Who sings for joy; who wonders, and who weeps;
It is the child in us at night who sleeps.
It is the child who silent turns his face,
Open and maskless, naked of defense,
Simple with trust, distilled of all pretense,
To sudden beauty in another's face—

It is the child in us who loves.

Alms

Like birds in winter
You fed me;
Knowing the ground was frozen,
Knowing
I should never come to your hand,
Knowing
You did not need my gratitude.

Softly,
Like snow falling on snow,
Softly, so not to frighten me,
Softly,
You threw your crumbs upon the ground —
And walked away.

The Little Mermaid
(After Hans Christian Andersen's story)

Only the little mermaid knows the price
One pays for mortal love, what sacrifice
Exacted by the Sea-Witch, should one choose
A mermaid's careless liberty to lose.

Into the smoky cauldron she must throw
A mermaid's kingdom, gleaming far below
The restless waves in filtered light that falls
Through dim pellucid depths on palace walls.

All childhood haunts must go, all memories;
Her swaying garden of anemones
Circled by conch-shells, where the sea-fans dance
To unheard music, bending in a trance.

No longer — now she seeks a mortal home —
Sharing with sisters laughter light as foam.
Those moon-bright nights alone upon the shore,
Singing a mermaid's song, are hers no more.

11

The magic sweetness of a mermaid's song,
She must abandon, if she would belong
To mortal world, the gift — O fatal choice —
That might have won the Prince, her golden voice.

The mermaid's silver tail, with which to dart
From octopi; the mermaid's coral heart
That felt no pain, she now must do without,
Exchanged for mortal longing, mortal doubt.

Even—

Him that I love I wish to be
Free:

Free as the bare top twigs of tree,
Pushed up out of the fight
Of branches, struggling for the light,
Clear of the darkening pall,
Where shadows fall—
Open to the golden eye
Of sky;

Free as a gull
Alone upon a single shaft of air,
Invisible there,
Where
No man can touch,
No shout can reach,
Meet
No stare;

Free as a spear
Of grass,

13

Lost in the green
Anonymity
Of a thousand seen
Piercing, row on row,
The crust of earth,
With mirth,
Through to the blue,
Sharing the sun
Although,
Circled, each one,
In his cool sphere
Of dew.

Him that I love, I wish to be
Free —
Even from me.

Two Citadels

We cannot meet, two citadels of stone
Imprisoned in our walls; two worlds that spin
Each in a separate orbit, each alone.
We are two homesteads, sheltering within
A score of lives. A score of household selves
Polish the floors, replenish pantry shelves,
Ticking to duties all the clock-told day,
Without a window-look across the way.

We cannot meet; stone citadels stand fast;
Two worlds do not embrace; homesteads are bound,
Attached to place, to time, to one day's round.
But evenings when the drudgery is past
And blinds are drawn and children safe in bed,
And adults sit and dream and nod the head,
A child within each house can slip apart,
Run barefoot down the stairs and out to meet
His playmate. Breathless, in the dark, they greet
And fling each other wholly heart to heart.

A Leaf, a Flower, and a Stone

Now there are no more words,
I bring a leaf, a flower, and a stone.

A leaf for my mouth
That can no longer speak,
Where you may trace
Along vein's laddered lace,
Graven as hieroglyph,
Thought's groping, tentative
But certain, toward your South:
A leaf for my mouth.

A flower for my heart
That finds no song;
Purer than rhyme,
Fragrance may climb,
Petal on petal,
Up the perfumed stair
To you, aware
Of music more profound,
More innocent than art:
A flower for my heart.

A stone for my hand
That silent comes to rest
Within your palm, a bird,
Hidden upon the nest,
Who, in a spiral, heard,
Mid-flight, the call
That sent its body small
Plummeting earthward, home,
Heavy with gravity
It cannot understand:
A stone for my hand.

Now there are no more words,
But you will know, when I sing
For others, that I bring
To you alone
A leaf, a flower, and a stone.

Interior Tree

Burning tree upon the hill
And burning tree within my heart,
What kinship stands between the two,
What cord I cannot tear apart?

The passionate gust that sets one free,
—A flock of leaves in sudden flight—
Shatters the bright interior tree
Into a shower of splintered light.

Fused moments of felicity,
When flame in eye and heart unite,
Come they from earth, or can they be
The swallows of eternity?

DEATH

A Final Cry

Praise life — Praise life —
Before the fall
Of winter's knife,
They stand and call,
O man, praise life.

The bee who goes
To the aster knows
December's fear;

The butterfly
On a daisy's eye,
That death is near;

Flies in the sun,
That summer's done;

Ripe berries wait
Their certain fate.

In red and gold
The lesson's told;

In ecstasy
The end foresee.

21

A final cry
From earth to sky,
Tree, fruit, and flower,
Before the hour
Of sacrifice:

Praise life, O man,
While yet you can.

No Angels

You think there are no angels any more —
No angels come to tell us in the night
Of joy or sorrow, love or death —
No breath of wings, no touch of palm to say
Divinity is near.
Today
Our revelations come
By telephone, or postman at the door,
You say —
        Oh no, the hour when fate is near,
Not these, the voices that can make us hear,
Not these
Have power to pierce below the stricken mind
Deep down into perception's quivering core.
Blows fall unheeded on the bolted door;
Deafly we listen; blindly look; and still
Our fingers fumbling with the lock are numb,
Until
The Angels come.

Oh, do you not recall
It was a tree,
Springing from earth so passionately straight

And tall,
That made you see, at last, what giant force
Lay pushing in your heart?
And was it not that spray
Of dogwood blossoms, white across your road,
That all at once made grief too great a load
To bear?

No angels any more, you say,
No towering sword, no angry seas divide —
No angels —
            But a single bud of quince,
Flowering out of season on the day
She died,
Cracked suddenly across a porcelain world!

Elegy Under the Stars

I here; you there —
But under those eyes, space is all-where.

I alive; you dead —
But under those eyes, all-time is spread.

I alone —
But under those eyes, all things are joined;
All sorrow, and all beauty, and all spirit,
Are one.

Testament

But how can I live without you? — she cried.

I left all world to you when I died:
Beauty of earth and air and sea;
Leap of a swallow or a tree;
Kiss of rain and wind's embrace;
Passion of storm and winter's face;
Touch of feather, flower, and stone;
Chiselled line of branch or bone;
Flight of stars, night's caravan;
Song of crickets — and of man —
All these I put in my testament,
All these I bequeathed you when I went.

But how can I see them without your eyes
Or touch them without your hand?
How can I hear them without your ear,
Without your heart, understand?

These too, these too
I leave to you!

Presence

I lift my head
    To find on high
A wheeling hawk
    Upon the sky —
        So far above,
        There too, my love?

Down at my feet
    A weed has pressed
Its scarlet knife
    Against my breast —
        O miracle,
        Are you here too?

Mountain

While you were there,
Some place, some where
Upon this planet's face,
Breath ran at swifter pace,
As if the air
Were lighter, rare,
Distilled as amber wine;
Alpine.

Now with your death
I find my burdened breath
An unaccustomed care,
Heavier by a hair
One scarce can see,
But breath's no luxury;
A feather more is all
To make lungs rise and fall,
Catastrophe.

So little change
That it seems strange
Without my mountain there

(Some place, some where)
I find the weight of air
Almost too great to bear.

All Saints' Day

Today no breath
  Of life's allowed
For Autumn spins
  Her silken shroud.

Thread upon thread
  The earth is bound
(November's needle
  Makes the round).

No wind may lift
  The fallen leaf,
No flower, split
  The face of grief.

No flight of birds
  Distracts the eye
Across the smooth
  Unravelled sky.

So still the day,
  So pure, so bare;
Imprisoned in
  Her crystal stare,

Earth waits a miracle —
  Man too;
This is the day
  All saints pass through.

Second Sowing

For whom
The milk ungiven in the breast
When the child is gone?

For whom
The love locked up in the heart
That is left alone?

That golden yield
Split sod once, overflowed an August field,
Threshed out in pain upon September's floor,
Now hoarded high in barns, a sterile store.

Break down the bolted door;
Rip open, spread and pour
The grain upon the barren ground
Wherever crack in clod is found.

There is no harvest for the heart alone;
The seed of love must be
Eternally
Resown.

CAPTIVE SPIRIT

"Closing In"

Just room for me to squeeze between
   The lowered ceiling and divide,
Just power enough to make the ridge
   And, panting, gain the other side;

Just light enough to see my field
   And in the shadows kiss the grass;
Just strength, just heart, just time enough,
   For me, the tardy one, to pass.

O hill, O strip of clearing sky,
   Hold up the bars till I get by!
O lovely day—forgive my sin,
   One breath of light will let me in!

Security

There is refuge in a sea-shell —
Or a star;
But in between,
Nowhere.

There is peace in the immense —
Or the small;
Between the two,
Not at all.

The planet in the sky,
The sea-shell on the ground:
And though all heaven and earth
                    between them lie,
No peace is to be found
Elsewhere.

Oh you who turn
For refuge, learn
From women, who have always known
The only roads that life has shown

To be secure.
How sure
The path a needle follows — or a star;
The near — the far.
With what compare
The light reflected from a thimble's stare,
Unless, on high,
Arcturus' eye?

The near — the far:
But in between,
Oh where
Is comfort to be seen?

There is refuge in a sea-shell —
Or a star;
But in between,
Nowhere.

Dogwood

The dogwood hurts me as I run
Beneath its load
This Spring,
Those white stars cascading
Down the wood road,
Those white blossoms with their faces
Upturned to the sun.

The grace of their branches is compassionate,
In an uncompassionate world.
The whiteness of their blossoms is too pure
To be unfurled
In a world soiled by the feet of men;
And they are open — too open,
In their flat uplifted acceptance
Of the sky.

Besides,
They lie.
They say —
(And I do not believe!)

They say—
(Oh, they deceive—they deceive!)
They say—
(And I shut my ears to their cry):

"Look, it is here, the answer,
It is here,
If you would only see,
If you would only listen,
If you would only open your heart."
They say—
"Look, it is here!"

No Harvest Ripening
Autumn 1939

Come quickly, winter, for the heart belies
The truth of these warm days. These August skies
Are all too fair to suit the times—so kind
That almost they persuade the treacherous mind
It still is summer and the world the same.
These gaudy colors on the hills in flame
Are out of keeping with the nun's attire
We wear within—of ashes, not of fire.

Season of ripening fruit and seeds, depart;
There is no harvest ripening in the heart.

Bring the frost that strikes the dahlias down
In one cruel night. The blackened buds, the brown
And wilted heads, the crippled stems, we crave—
All beauty withered, crumbling to the grave.
Wind, strip off the leaves, and harden, Ground,
Till in your frozen crust no break is found.

Then only, when man's inner world is one
With barren earth and branches bared to bone,
Then only can the heart begin to know
The seeds of hope asleep beneath the snow;
Then only can the chastened spirit tap
The hidden faith still pulsing in the sap.

Only with winter-patience can we bring
The deep-desired, long-awaited spring.

The Stone

There is a core of suffering that the mind
Can never penetrate or even find;
A stone that clogs the stream of my delight,
Hidden beneath the surface out of sight,
Below the flow of words it lies concealed.
It blocks my passage and it will not yield
To hammer blows of will, and still resists
The surgeon's scalpel of analysis.
Too hard for tears and too opaque for light,
Bright shafts of prayer splinter against its might.
Beauty cannot disguise nor music melt
A pain undiagnosable but felt.

No sleep dissolves that stony stalagmite
Mounting within the unconscious caves of night.

No solvent left but love. Whose love? My own?
And is one asked to love the harsh unknown?
I am no Francis who could kiss the lip
Of alien leper. Caught within the grip

Of world un-faith, I cannot even pray,
And must I love? Is there no other way?

Suffering without name or tongue or face,
Blindly I crush you in my dark embrace!

Pilgrim

This is a road
  One walks alone;
Narrow the track
  And overgrown.

Dark is the way
  And hard to find,
When the last village
  Drops behind.

Never a footfall
  Light to show
Fellow traveller —
  Yet I know

Someone before
  Has trudged his load
In the same footsteps —
  This is a road.

Saint for Our Time

("... But at last he made his way to the other bank, and set the child down, saying: 'Child, thou hast put me in dire peril, and hast weighed so heavy upon me that if I had borne the whole world upon my shoulders, it could not have burdened me more heavily!' And the child answered: 'Wonder not, Christopher, for not only hast thou borne the whole world upon thy shoulders, but Him Who created the world'...."
The Golden Legend)

Christopher, come back to earth again.
There is no age in history when men
So cried for you, Saint of a midnight wild,
Who stood beside a stream and heard a child.
Not even Francis, brother to the poor,
Who, barefoot, begged for alms from door to door,
And pity-tortured kissed the leper's brow —
Not even Francis is so needed now
As you, Christ-bearer.
                              Christopher, we die
Not for our lack of charity; we lie
Imprisoned in our sepulchers of stone,
Wanting your gift, O Saint, your gift alone.

45

No one will take the burden of the whole
Upon his shoulders; each man in his soul
Thinks his particular grief too great to bear
Without demanding still another's share.

But you—you chose to bear a brother's load
And every man who travelled down your road
You ferried on your back across the flood
Until one night beside the stream there stood,
Wrapped in a cloak of storm, a child who cried
And begged safe passage to the other side—
A child who weighed upon your back like lead,
Like earth upon the shoulders of the dead—
And, struggling to the bank while torrents whirled,
You found that on your shoulder leaned a world.

No wonder that the burden was so great:
You carried in your arms the monstrous weight

46

Of all men's happiness and all men's pain,
And all men's sorrows on your back had lain.
Even their sins you carried as your own—
Even their sins, you, Christopher, alone!

But who today will take the risk or blame
For someone else? Everyone is the same,
Dreading his neighbor's tongue or pen or deed.
Imprisoned in fear we stand and do not heed
The cry that you once heard across the stream.
"There is no cry," we say, "it is a dream."

Christopher, the waters rise again,
As on that night, the waters rise; the rain
Bites like a whip across a prisoner's back;
The lightning strikes like fighters in attack;
And thunder, like a time-bomb, detonates
The starless sky no searchlight penetrates.

The child is crying on the further shore:
Christopher, come back to earth once more.

THE UNICORN

The Unicorn in Captivity

(After the tapestry in The Cloisters)

Here sits the Unicorn
In captivity;
His bright invulnerability
Captive at last;
The chase long past,
Winded and spent,
By the king's spears rent;
Collared and tied
To a pomegranate tree —
Here sits the Unicorn
In captivity,
Yet free.

Here sits the Unicorn;
His overtakelessness
Bound by a circle small
As a maid's embrace;
Ringed by a round corral;
Pinioned in place
By a fence of scarlet rail,
Fragile as a king's crown,
Delicately laid down

Over horn, hoofs, and tail,
As a butterfly net
Is lightly set.

He could leap the corral,
If he rose
To his full white height;
He could splinter the fencing light,
With three blows
Of his porcelain hoofs in flight—
If he chose.
He could shatter his prison wall,
Could escape them all—
If he rose,
If he chose.

Here sits the Unicorn;
The wounds in his side
Still bleed
From the huntsmen's spears,
Yet he takes no heed
Of the blood-red tears

On his milk-white hide,
That spring unsealed,
Like flowers that rise
From the velvet field
In which he lies.
Dream wounds, dream ties,
Do not bind him there
In a kingdom where
He is unaware
Of his wounds, of his snare.

Here sits the Unicorn;
Head in a collar cased,
Like a girdle laced
Round a maiden's waist,
Broidered and buckled wide,
Carelessly tied.
He could slip his head
From the jewelled noose
So lightly tied —
If he tried,
As a maid could loose
The belt from her side;

He could slip the bond
So lightly tied —
If he tried.

Here sits the Unicorn;
Leashed by a chain of gold
To the pomegranate tree.
So light a chain to hold
So fierce a beast;
Delicate as a cross at rest
On a maiden's breast.
He could snap the golden chain
With one toss of his mane,
If he chose to move,
If he chose to prove
His liberty.
But he does not choose
What choice would lose.
He stays, the Unicorn,
In captivity.

In captivity,
Flank, hoofs, and mane —

Yet look again—
His horn is free,
Rising above
Chain, fence, and tree,
Free hymn of love;
His horn
Bursts from his tranquil brow,
Like a comet born;
Cleaves like a galley's prow
Into seas untorn;
Springs like a lily, white
From the earth below;
Spirals, a bird in flight
To a longed-for height;
Or a fountain bright,
Spurting to light
Of early morn—
O luminous horn!

Here sits the Unicorn—
In captivity?
In repose.
Forgotten now the blows

When the huntsmen rose
With their spears; dread sounds
Of the baying hounds,
With their cry for blood;
And the answering flood
In his veins for strife,
Of his rage for life,
In hoofs that plunged,
In horn that lunged.
Forgotten the strife;
Now the need to kill
Has died like fire,
And the need to love
Has replaced desire;
Forgotten now the pain
Of the wounds, the fence, the chain, —
Where he sits so still,
Where he waits Thy will.

Quiet, the Unicorn,
In contemplation stilled,
With acceptance filled;

Quiet, save for his horn;
Alive in his horn;
Horizontally,
In captivity;
Perpendicularly,
Free.
As prisoners might,
Looking on high at night,
From day-close discipline
Of walls and bars,
To night-free infinity
Of sky and stars,
Find here felicity:
So is he free —
The Unicorn.
What is liberty?
Here lives the Unicorn,
In captivity,
Free.

OPEN SKY

Space

For beauty, for significance, it's space
We need; and since we have no space today
In which to frame the act, the word, the face
Of beauty, it's no longer beautiful.

A tree's significant when it's alone,
Standing against the sky's wide open face;
A sail, spark-white upon the space of sea,
Can pin a whole horizon into place.

Encompassed by the dark, a candle flowers,
Creating space around it as it towers,
Giving the room a shape, a form, a name;
Significance is born within the frame.

A word falls in the silence like a star,
Searing the empty heavens with the scar
Of beautiful and solitary flight
Against the dark and speechless space of night.

Winter Tree

Again the oak, bare, stripped and barren, brings
More confirmation to the heart than Spring's
Returning green; more courage to refind
The winter-bones of spirit unobscured
By summer-flesh of leaves. The troubled mind
After the Fall's deception, reassured—
After the wind, after the winter storm—
By deep return to discipline of form.

What power hidden in the winter tree
Can set the captive spirit running free,
Following vault of trunk and leap of limb,
Singing through fountain of the branch a hymn,
Spilling through laughter of the twigs in flight
Out to the limitless expanse of light?

Does mortal eye, so trained by mortal frame,
Find in the tree's uplifted boughs the same
Gesture of supplication or of praise
We mortals use, when mortal arms we raise?

Or does the adult mind, remembering
The child's conception of the sky, still cling
To images of God who sits on high?
(We too might reach Him, could we touch the sky!)

Or does the startled spirit recognize
A deeper kinship that the mind denies,
Within the skeletal form of tree concealed,
Symbol of its own struggle find revealed;
A form so contrapuntal and yet pure;
The chosen path, fortuitous, yet sure;
The thrust, the spread, the lift, apparently
So free, and yet tap-rooted in the ground;
The shape, an individual, yet bound
By its generic law: it is a tree.

Does spirit see—even recall, somehow,
The tortured path that's taken by the bough,
Remember as its own, no need to learn,
Each thrust and block and compensating turn
The sap must make in its slow odyssey,
Journey from trunk to twig, from earth to sky?

63

And does the pattern here not clarify,
Perceived at last in its entirety,
A confirmation of essential trend;
Assurance that the tree does in the end,
In its slow pilgrimage from root to flower,
Pulsing with all of sap's blind, patient power —
Power of faith, of prayer, of prophecy —
Reach in the polar buds the open sky?

Pas de deux—Winter

Caught in a silver spell this kingdom lies,
Enchanted like the Sleeping Beauty's world,
Where clocks are faceless and where flags are furled,
Where page and princess droop with bud-closed eyes,
Waiting the touch of man to come to flower.
The skier is the prince who brings the power
Of life and motion; he alone can pass,
Spanning with feet of flame, the steep crevasse.
He scales the crystal mountain, dares to ride
The dragon of the snows to claim his bride,
Shattering the frozen breath of palace hall,
To wake the marble princess from her thrall,
Winning a partner for his frenzied skill,
He dances with the diamond-hearted hill.

Ascent

Plunge deep
Into the sky
O wing
Of the soul.

Reach
Past the last pinnacle
Of speech
Into the vast
Inarticulate face
Of silence.

Outleap
The turbulent gust
From forest,
Or the dust
Spiralling from the plain,
A yellow stain,
Swiftly erased again
In traceless tracts
Of space.

Up, up beyond
The giddy peaks of fear,
The glacial fields of doubt,
The sheer
Cliffs of despair;

Climb the steep stair
Of air.
There,
Where the gimlet screw
Of height-driven hawk
Pierces the blue,
Pursue!

There,
Where the wing
Has ceased to beat
For its own
Victory or defeat,

Find,
Far behind
The pale cloud-pastures
Of the mind,

67

The unbroken blind
Brightness of sheer
Atmosphere.

Here, crystalline,
Deep, full, serene,
Here flows
The still, unfathomed river
Of repose.

Here out of sight,
Unseen but known,
Here glides the stream
Of compassion.
Here alone
May rest
The strangled breast
Of long-impassioned flight.

Here soar
With more than wing
Above earth's floor;
Here ride

Limitless on a tide
No hawk has ever tried.

Here turn
In marble-firm
Security;
Here learn
To pivot on a needle-point —
Eternity.

Here whole
At last, above
The halting flight
That blindly rose
To gain a hidden height,

Wing of the soul
Repose,
Serene
In the stream
Of Love.

Flight of Birds

Watching the patterns of these birds in flight,
Fluid as music on a page and white
As falling petals, I find swift escape.
Then all at once my life takes sudden shape,
And I can understand the misprized art
Of reading palms or tea leaves in a cup;
Remember wise men searching in the skies,
Looking for omens in the tracks of birds,
Telling the future in cloud-darkened lines.

It is not fate in these external signs
We read; it is ourselves—ourselves we see,
Transmuted into bird or cloud or tree,
Familiar fragments, here arranged in form;
As a kaleidoscope contains the power
From common specks and straws to make a flower.

Act of creation in which the stone,
The sculptor, and the spectator, are one—
Here, where the art and artist coincide,
Where universe and private world collide,
Magic of mandala and Rorschach meet;

And childhood memories again repeat
Who loses life shall gain it—Miracle
The heart reborn upon a flight of birds
Can now accept and recognize in words.

Back to the Islands

Here on the mainland I am rooted down,
Tethered to earth's four corners like a barn,
Balanced to bear the seasons as they ride,
Hay-carts and cattle, grain and crops, in stride.
Square to the world, I watch the sun's slow pace,
Morning and evening, from my steadfast place.

But when I leave the mainland and I go
Back to the islands where the waters flow
In unpredicted paths, and landmarks shift
With rudder angle or a full sail's lift,
My firm Newtonian universe dissolves,
And in my heart the compass rose revolves.

As Bach once played upon a folk-worn song,
Tide, wind, and water counterpoint among
Familiar granite slabs until they seem
No longer static, borne upon a stream,
As seagulls on a shaft of air in flight;

Or boats — white sides, pine-masted — pulling tight
Against their anchors, waiting for the right
Touch to raise sails, go scudding out of sight.

And I — I feel my pattern too might change,
Living among the islands; all is strange —
A bay, a cove, a sudden turn of tide,
An unexpected channel never tried
Before. Time and the mainland stand aside
Once more — Once more, life shatters open wide!

WIND OF TIME

Presentiment

I am still as an autumn tree
In which there is no wind,
No breath of movement—yet
There on a top branch,
For no cause I can see,
A single leaf oscillates
Violently.

To what thin melody
Does it dance?
What lost note vibrates
In me?
From the past or the future?
Memory
Or Presentiment?

Within the Wave

Within the hollow wave there lies a world,
Gleaming glass-perfect, rising to be hurled
Into a thousand fragments on the sand,
Driven by tide's inexorable hand.
Now in the instant while disaster towers,
I glimpse a land more beautiful than ours;
Another sky, more lapis-lazuli,
Lit by unsetting suns; another sea
By no horizon bound; another shore,
Glistening with shells I never saw before.
Smooth mirror of the present, poised between
The crest's "becoming" and the foam's "has been" —
How luminous the landscape seen across
The crystal lens of an impending loss!

Family Album

(On a photograph of my father and mother just married)

My parents, my children:
Who are you, standing there
In an old photograph—young married pair
I never saw before, yet see again?
You pose somewhat sedately side by side,
In your small yard off the suburban road.
He stretches a little in young manhood's pride
Broadening his shoulders for the longed-for load,
The wife that he has won, a home his own;
His growing powers hidden as spring, unknown,
But surging in him toward their certain birth,
Explosive as dandelions in the earth.

She leans upon his arm, as if to hide
A strength perhaps too forward for a bride,
Feminine in her bustle and long skirt;
She looks demure, with just a touch of flirt
In archly tilted head and squinting smile
At the photographer, she watches while
Pretending to be girl, although so strong,
Playing the role of wife ("Here I belong!"),

Anticipating mother, with man for child,
Amused at all her roles, unreconciled.

And I who gaze at you and recognize
The budding gestures that were soon to be
My cradle and my home, my trees, my skies,
I am your child, staring at you with eyes
Of love and grief for parents who have died;
But also with omniscience born of time,
Seeing your unlined faces, dreams untried,
Your tentativeness and your brave attack,
I am no longer daughter gazing back;
I am your mother, watching far ahead,
Seeing events so clearly now they're gone
And both of you are dead, and I alone,
And in my own life now already past
That garden in the grass where you two stand.

I long to comfort you for all you two
In time to come must meet and suffer through,
To answer with a hindsight-given truth
The questions in those wondering eyes of youth.

I long to tell you, starting on your quest,
"You'll do it all, you know, you'll meet the test."

Mother compassionate and child bereft
I am; the past and present, wisdom and innocence,
Fused by one flicker of a camera lens
Some stranger snapped in laughter as he left
More than a half a century ago —
My children, my parents.

Broken Shell

Cease searching for the perfect shell, the whole
Inviolate form no tooth of time has cracked;
The alabaster armor still intact
From sand's erosion and the breaker's roll.

What can we salvage from the ocean's strife
More lovely than these skeletons that lie
Like scattered flowers open to the sky,
Yet not despoiled by their consent to life?

The pattern on creation morning laid,
By softened lip and hollow, unbetrayed;
The gutted frame endures, a testament,
Even in fragment, to that first intent.

Look at this spiral, stripped to polished nerve
Of growth. Erect as compass in its curve,
It swings forever to the absolute,
Crying out beauty like a silver flute.

Revisitation

You have been dead for months; the daylight mind
Has noted in its record the exact
Moment of dying, has transferred the fact
To its dream-counterpart — the shadowy pool
Where all events are mirrored upside down,
Distorted but more vivid than by day —
That nowhere on this earth can you be found;
Not here, not there, nor on a journey bound
From which you'll soon be back. Not just away,
But gone "for good," you are.
                              Even though I know,
And grief is past and life goes on — even so,
Still I must make a faithful pilgrimage
To those particular landmarks that were yours,
Or intimately haunted by your sight;
Not in the hope of finding you again,
Not in obeisance to your memory,
Nor self-indulgently in search of pain.

No, I must go
Back to the places where you put your hand,
To see them now without you, gutted, bare,

Swept hollow of your presence. I must stand
Alone and in their empty faces stare,
To find another truth I do not know;
To balance those unequal shifted planes
Of our existence, yours and mine; to fix
The whirling landscapes of the heart in which
I walk a stranger both to space and time.

I must go back;
In each familiar corner wait until
I witness once again the flesh turn cold,
The spirit parting from the body's hold;
And let it go, and love the landscape still;
But now on only for itself alone,
As you once loved it when, in flesh and bone,
You walked it first, naked of memories,
And sharp with life, you loved its flesh and bone.
For I must meet and marry in myself
The truth of what has ended, what is new;
The past and future; death and life. And when
At last the two conflicting pairs are met;

The planes are balanced and the landscapes set;
The strands of past and future tied in one
Tough, weather-beaten, salted twist of hemp,
The present — Then
I shall be able to refind myself,
And also, you.

Bare Tree

Already I have shed the leaves of youth,
Stripped by the wind of time down to the truth
Of winter branches. Linear and alone
I stand, a lens for lives beyond my own,
A frame through which another's fire may glow,
A harp on which another's passion, blow.

The pattern of my boughs, an open chart
Spread on the sky, to others may impart
Its leafless mysteries that once I prized,
Before bare roots and branches equalized;
Tendrils that tap the rain or twigs the sun
Are all the same; shadow and substance one.
Now that my vulnerable leaves are cast aside,
There's nothing left to shield, nothing to hide.

Blow through me, Life, pared down at last to bone,
So fragile and so fearless have I grown!